CORAL SNAKES

AMAZING SNAKES

Ted O'Hare

Rourke
Publishing LLC
Vero Beach, Florida 32964

www.rourkepublishing.com

PHOTO CREDITS: Title page, pp. 8, 10, 21 © James H. Carmichael; cover, pp. 7, 18, 19 © Lynn M. Stone; pp. 12, 15 © George Van Horn; page 17 © Michael Fogden/Bruce Coleman

Title Page: *The eastern coral snake lives from North Carolina south through Florida and into Louisiana, Texas, and Mexico.*

Editor: Frank Sloan

Cover and interior design by Nicola Stratford

Library of Congress Cataloging-in-Publication Data

O'Hare, Ted, 1961-
   Coral snakes / Ted O'Hare.
       p. cm. -- (Amazing snakes)
   Includes bibliographical references and index.
   ISBN 1-59515-142-7 (hardcover)
   1. Coral snakes--Juvenile literature. I. Title. II. Series: O'Hare, Ted, 1961-
Amazing snakes.
   QL666.O64O4 2004
   597.96'44--dc22
                                    2004008013

Printed in the USA

CG/CG

table of contents

coral Snakes

Coral snakes are members of the *Elapidae* family. Like all snakes, they are **reptiles**. There are more than 70 **species** of coral snakes, and they all contain **venom**.

Coral snakes can be identified by their red, yellow, and black bands. The eastern coral snake has its red and yellow colors side by side.

The eastern coral snake of the United States is just one kind of coral snake found in North, Central, and South America.

where they Live

Coral snakes live in North, Central, and South America. They don't live anywhere else in the world. Only the Texas, Sonoran, and eastern coral snakes are found in the United States.

The Sonoran coral snake likes a warm, dry climate. The eastern coral snake often lies under dead vegetation near water. South American coral snakes like to live under the bark of trees.

The Sonoran coral snake lives in Arizona, Mexico, and the southwest corner of New Mexico.

what they Look Like

All coral snakes have slim bodies with blunt heads and tiny eyes. The adults are about 2 feet (less than 1 meter) long. Coral snakes have smooth, glossy scales. The bodies are patterned with bands of two or three colors. Most species of coral snakes have some black on their heads.

Did you Know?

Some South American coral snakes are more than 5 feet (1.5 m) long.

Coral snakes have black heads and glossy scales.

their Senses

The coral snake relies on its sense of smell to find **prey**. The coral snake flicks its tongue and brings in particles. The **Jacobson's organ** in the snake's mouth analyzes the nearby particles.

The coral snake cannot see well, but it can detect nearby movement. The snake also feels ground **vibration**. This helps the snake identify enemies, and it is able to escape.

The coral snake hunts by using its tongue to sense things around it.

11

Nostril

Fangs

Windpipe

Tongue

the Head and Mouth

The coral snake's small head has a blunt nose. Short fangs are at the front of the upper jaw. The snake has venom glands located behind each eye. Muscles around these glands pump venom from the glands to the snake's victims.

Coral snakes and their cousins do not have hollow fangs as the other venomous snakes of North America do.

The venom **paralyzes** the prey. The coral snake stretches its jaws like a rubber band. It then swallows the victim whole. While the snake swallows its prey, its windpipe increases in size so the snake can keep breathing.

A coral snake's bite kills another snake.

Baby coral Snakes

In the summer the mother coral snake lays 6 to 12 eggs. She lays them in vegetation that will give warmth and humidity, so the eggs can grow. After about two months, the eggs hatch brightly colored babies. As soon as they are born, the babies can kill prey and defend themselves.

A baby coral snake crawls from its eggshell in Costa Rica.

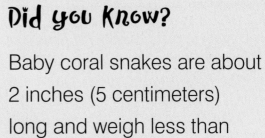

Did you know?

Baby coral snakes are about 2 inches (5 centimeters) long and weigh less than half an ounce.

Did you know?
Birds and many small animals eat the coral snake.

their prey

Coral snakes hunt prey during the daytime. Lizards and other snakes are the prey of coral snakes. Most coral snakes will even eat their look-alike, the scarlet kingsnake. Scientists think that many **predators** recognize the coral snake's bright colors and stay away.

The red-shouldered hawk is a predator of coral snakes in the southeastern United States.

The scarlet kingsnake is one of many non-venomous snakes that look much like coral snakes.

their Defense

Most coral snakes hide as a defense. The snakes move swiftly across the dead vegetation of the forest floor. This makes them difficult to see.

Did you know?

When threatened, the coral snake hides its head under its tail. This confuses the enemy, and the snake may be able to escape.

Coral snakes spend much of their lives hidden in forest leaves and litter.

coral Snakes and People

The coral snake has **toxic** venom. People in the southeastern United States fear this creature. But because the snake is so small, the venom does not usually cause death to humans. The coral snake is shy and is therefore not likely to bite.

Glossary

Jacobson's organ (JAYK ub sunz ORG un) — the part of a snake that analyzes a scent the snake has picked up

paralyzes (PAR uh lie zez) — causes loss of movement to an object

predators (PRED uh turz) — animals that hunt and kill other animals for food

prey (PRAY) — animals hunted and killed by other animals for food

reptiles (REP TYLZ) — animals with cold blood, a backbone, and scales or plates

species (SPEE sheez) — a certain kind of plant or animal within a closely related group

toxic (TOCK sick) — extremely poisonous

venom (VEN um) — poisonous matter that some snakes use to injure or kill

vibration (VY bray shun) — movement that can be experienced

index

Further Reading

"Coral Snake." International Wildlife Encyclopedia, vol. 4. Cavendish, 2002.
Feldman, Heather. *Coral Snakes*. PowerKids, 2004.
Solway, Andrew. *Deadly Snakes*. Heinemann Library, 2004.

Websites to Visit

www.desertusa.com/mag98/may/papr/du_westcoral.html
www.ladywildlife.com/animal/coralsnake.html
www.wf.net/~snake/coral.htm

About the Author

Ted O'Hare is an author and editor of children's nonfiction books. He divides his time between New York City and a home upstate.